FOUR TO TWELVE

YOHAN

PublishAmerica

Baltimore

Hardcover 9781462675784
PUBLISHED BY PUBLISHAMERICA, LLLP
www.publishamerica.com
Baltimore

Printed in the United States of America

FOUR TO TWELVE

When I contemplated writing this story a few pro's and con's surfaced in my anxious mind. I debated wether this would be a good path to tread. Would I be reopening old wounds? Creating new ones? Would this be a trigger? The decision was made for me.

First a little background. I am by no means 'Holier-than-thou' and really despise people who preach from their self-righteous soap boxes. Nothing annoys me more. Often, when giving an opinion or piece of advice concerning drug addiction I am rebuffed with the usual. "You're no better" or "People in glass houses..." Does this mean I should remain silent and not give the Ha... Benefit of my experiences? I considered thoughts along this route and decided to write as a positive tool and if along the way I can help even one person, I'd ease my karmic debt.

A bit of background. I'm a middle aged guy from a lower-middle class family residing in the mid west some thirty miles from a major city in the suburbs. I am the eldest of three children. Two of whom are modestly successful in their chosen fields. My father was/is an alcoholic from a long line of alcoholics. The type of alcoholics that don't get hangovers and are free to wallow in their poison of choice without physical ramifications. At least for the first twenty, thirty years. My mother is a hearing impaired woman with a big heart and a sucker for lost causes. More about them later.

I guess my introduction to illicit substances began in my early teens. I started smoking cigarettes and remember how much I hated them but they were a ticket into a clique where I felt welcome. Peer pressure? To be sure, part of a group nonetheless. In retrospect I think I was responding to my gradual hearing loss. It got to the point where it became noticeable. My new friends thought this was hilarious and marveled at the skill of lip reading. It was nice to be at the top of the food chain. Had I known then, what I know now, I would've warned myself that Misery LOVES company.

The years passed and I went through the various stages, various substances of dependency and abuse. Alcohol being the biggest gateway drug. The last stop was cocaine/ alcohol. What to say about cocaine? A substance that completely erases all physical and mental pain/worries In 8 seconds to 15 minutes, depending on the delivery system. You feel reborn, re-energized, That is until you've used it awhile. This fountain of youth was quickly overshadowed by horrendous nosebleeds and physical hangovers that would last for days. It was then I switched to a new delivery system and probably the most dangerous. Smoking crack. Here is where my story begins...

PRELUDE

"You need to turn yourself in Friday at Six P.M." The officer said in matter of fact voice. It was six weeks after being arrested. A friend and I had gone to buy 20$ worth of crack. It was a Thursday afternoon. The usual run, pull into a parking lot and wait for the dealer to drive by. Follow him around the corner, make the buy and leave. Simple enough. Until I saw flashing lights in my rear-view mirror. "We're being pulled over". I said to my partner in crime. "You're kidding" He replied. He then shoved the small bag into the air conditioning vent. Anyone who does drugs knows this is a no-no. There are no atheists in fox holes. "Don't put it in the air vent!" I said. 'We're fucked' I'm thinking. Play it cool I told myself. Maybe it's nothing. I pull over. The policeman gets out and walks up to the window. I roll it down. "Driver's license and insurance card" He says flatly. "Why aren't you wearing your seatbelt"? He inquires. "I am" I point out. Flexing the seatbelt proudly. I look over to my buddy and see to my horror, he is not. The officer goes back to his vehicle, runs our names. "I have a warrant" My buddy confesses. Great, now the officer can tell us to exit the vehicle. Another squad car arrives on the scene.

'We're fucked' I'm thinking...

The officer comes back and says "How do you know <persons name >?" "I don't know anyone by that name officer" Which was the truth. Never heard the name before. "CCccccccc?!" The officer shouts. That name I know. He's our dealer. "Mind if I search your car"? The officer says politely. I put on my best poker face. All in. "Go ahead". "I have nothing to hide". He radios again and a K-9 unit rolls up. 'We're fucked' I think again and again.

The holding cell in the police station slams shut. Six hours later an undercover cop escorts me to his office. He finger prints me and takes my mug shot. Not the ink and paper they used in the old days but a new high tech scanner. Much more accurate.

I'm put into another cell for an hour or so. "God do I need a cigarette" I think to myself.

After what seems like forever he returns and offers me a deal. I reply that I don't really know the guy and he says they need me to get the guy to sell out of his house. Later I find out that if the cops can get the guy selling out of his house they can get a John Doe warrant and seize his property/belongings. I honestly tell the policeman that this guy NEVER sells out of his house and to even suggest such a thing would expose me as a rat.

"You have till Tuesday to come up with something" He says. "Till then you're free to go". My accomplice and I are released. I get in my car noticing the cops have torn it apart. Guess they didn't believe that 20$ worth was all we had. We discuss our options on the way home and agree. Ratting isn't an option. We're fucked seems to have become my mantra. I am advised in the next few days by veterans of the penal system to 'Get my whites ready' Meaning they don't allow colored underwear in jail. Tuesday passes and turns into six weeks and just when we think they forgot about us. They call.

DAY 1

I am put into a holding cell after having to surrender my shoelaces. Odd that they wanted my shoelaces. The officer clangs the cell shut. That rumor stating that you don't really acknowledge being in jail until you hear that cell slam shut is absolutely true. Shortly thereafter an officer brings a clipboard for me to sign and I am horrified to see I am being charged with multiple felonies including an X felony. No wonder they take your shoelaces. "What the hell is this"? I demand to know. "It just acknowledges that you understand what you're being charged with". He replies flatly. Delivery of a controlled substance within a thousand feet of a church, park or school. This is insane. I'm no drug dealer. Later we are served stale sandwiches from a local store. Probably the same one we did the deal in. It tastes like sandpaper. I lay down in the brightly lit cell on my cot. Which is actually just a metal plate. The pillow is a plastic sandbag filled with sand. The next morning I'm shipped off to bond court in handcuffs that are way too tight. More than one night in that cell would kill a person. My cigarettes are confiscated and we head into bond court. I am relieved to see my sister and her boyfriend waiting in the aisles. I'm hearing impaired and most of what is said escapes me. I hear the words 7500.00 spoken and assuming I only need 10% I figure my sister can afford 750.00. No need to pay the mortgage this month right? I'm rushed out of the courtroom and the Saturday morning crowd is given one cigarette from the confiscated pile. I see my ultra-ultra lights and hesitate quickly deciding on the strongest brand visible. Had I known at the time how long processing would be I would've patted myself on the back.

A couple hours later we're all handcuffed together and ordered to board the bus. Having never been through this process made it interesting to observe when I could push the fear of uncertainty to the back of my mind. We drove some 10 miles or so to the county jail and as we rolled through the gate reality washed over me like a tsunami.

HELL. The only word that accurately describes this place. Recent conversations come to mind of advice offered from hardened criminals I had gotten high with recently. A few of them had done years in penitenteries. All of them said they'd rather do hard time there than this place. At the time I thought maybe they were messing with me... Not anymore.

We're ordered off the bus and walk down a long embankment. We're then ushered into the first of many holding pens. Christ on a cracker it stinks in here. I look over at the toilet and see its covered in feces, vomit and other unrecognizable fluids. Everyone starts to relax a little and sporadic conversations break out. What seems like hours pass and we're then herded into a large area with sections of chain link fence. Hundreds of people are here being processed. There is no where to sit comfortably. People are shoulder to shoulder. I see my accomplice. He's a pretty big guy and he muscles a couple spots for us to sit. "We'll be outta here at midnight". "They release drug criminals because of over-crowding". He states knowingly. Man, I hope so. This place SUCKS.

I keep repeating to myself ill be bailed out and just to hold it together till then. Theres a few men walking around obviously in need of psych medication. One guy starts to harass another to his surprise and he shouts "Hey man just leave me alone! Did I mess with you?" They continue to shout and push until a guard walks over and raps the fence.

Hours pass. We're relocated again and again until we reach the Medical screening . The dreaded Q-tip.

Ive heard many stories of the Syphillis screen. None of them good. I'm screened for TB and asked a multitude of questions concerning my sexual history and drug abuse history and gang affiliation. NO Q-TIP. I'm told later that the screening was suspended due to a large class action lawsuit against the jail citing harm. How ironic. Thank god for little favors. We're finally given our phone call and I dial my sister at my brothers house knowing theres a party going on. I put it together. She answers and I ask why I'm still in jail. Why hasn't she bailed me out? It was only 750.00$ I state earnestly. "NO she replies your bond was 75,000$ and 7500.00 was needed to bail you out." I still refuse to believe and I think I actually threatened to burn her house down before I slammed the receiver down. 'I'm fucked'...

I'm eventually led off to a much smaller holding area. A cell by the looks of it. We're packed into this little cell shoulder to shoulder. Its stifling hot. People start to get angry and yelling ensues. Barbaric is all I can think. Treated worse than animals. Ten of us are led out of this stifling oven and led down a dank hallway. We're ordered to strip. I notice female guards standing with male guards. No time to be modest. We're ordered to turn around and press our heads against the wall. Thank god he's yelling or I'd never understand what he's saying. The guy next to me takes his head an inch or two off the wall as he looks down the row and immediately his head is slammed against the concrete. He falls like a sack of potatoes. He's dragged away and I don't see him again till I'm released. Next we're told to bend over and spread our ass cheeks. How embaressing. I'd hate to have his job. The officer inspects our asses and were told to get dressed before being corralled into another building. We walk through the courtyard. The cool air feels heavenly. We enter another building and are stripped again. Only white underwear and navy blue underwear are allowed. The underwear must contain a fly. Were issued our DOC scrubs and sent to another building where were stripped again before being sent to dorms. I climb a few flights of stairs. Alone. I step through a heavy metal door. It's almost pitch black. A man steps out from behind the door and states I must shower. Looking back I can see the relevance. I've just spent many many hours in some pretty filthy surroundings. Warning bells go off inside my head and every rape scene I've ever seen on T.V. races through my head. I brace myself as I enter the bathroom. What to do with my hearing aids? I take the fastest shower of my life, thankfully still intact rectally. Its been 33 hours since I turned myself in.

I lay down on my cot and fall asleep.

DAY 2

I wake to the sound of a guard yelling to get in line. I jump up off my steel cot and walk over and get in line but am stopped by a white guy who bunks a few cots from me. He explains that the row of cots on the right side of the dorm go first, the left 2nd and the middle last. He tells me the name of the gangs and informs me we are 'Neutrons' meaning non-affiliated with gangs. Our middle row has a majority of white guys and the two gangs on either side are African Americans with a few white guys peppered in. We go to breakfast and the food is horrible. In fact a movie quote comes to mind of the 'breakfast' we are eating. I try not to smile and return to the dorm when finished. I'm given shower sandals that are 3x too big and trade my few snacks for a couple of home rolled smokes. No filtered cigarettes here. I smoke a cigarette like it was heaven sent, treasuring every puff and smoking it so low my fingers burn.

I head over to the drinking fountain and read the list of 'rules' posted above it.

1. No T.V. until you've spent ten days 'on deck' (Incarcerated, well that fkn sucks. Good thing I can

read lips and the T.v. Is close enough for me to see their mouths)

2.   Shower shoes must be worn in the shower

3.   Do not drink from the fountain w/out a cup

4.   One man at a time in the shower (Thank god)

I trade my last snack for a cup and return to my cot with a cold glass of water. I wonder to myself how the hell I got here. The hours pass oh so slowly and night sets in.

Definitely a different vibe in this place when night sets in. I look out the windows, many are broken or in need of repair behind the iron screen. No wonder its so damn cold in here. Cant even imagine how bad it would be in the winter. I'm told the jail is kept cold deliberately to minimize the violence. Brilliant. A few people question me as to why I'm here. They all state my 'crime' is a class 4 felony/possession and dismiss the class x and class one counts. I'm not reassured.

The leader of the gang to my left walks up and asks if I want some rocks. Code for crack. I'm nervous and without thinking answer 'sure'. He smiles and walks off.

I follow his movement with my eyes only till he reaches the only white guy in his gang. The white guy looks at me from across the room and shakes his head no as if he can't believe how stupid I am. I'm alarmed. A couple minutes later I get up and walk over to the 'boss' and tell him "You know what. Never mind I'll pass. Not in here". I later find out that my ass literally and figuratively was in jeapordy . NEVER owe anyone for anything in jail. I go back to my bunk and lie down. Two guys in the adjoining bunks ask me if I want to read from the Bible with them. I reply 'No, but I'll listen'. I close my eyes and am lulled to sleep to verses of a god I didn't believe in.

DAY 3

After breakfast I chat with a couple of guys in the middle row and try to pass the brain numbing slowness of the day. We're informed after lunch that prisoners who want to qualify for home arrest should form a line. I get up. Surely this is an answer to my half-assed prayers. We're stripped and searched before being escorted to another wing of the jail. The 'cell' is made of four sides of bars. Like the monkey cage at a zoo. I see a kid who looks like he's 15 weeping to himself 'I wanna go home' over and over. This is no place to show weakness. At all. He must've had a rough night. Better him than me. This unexpected thought surprises me since I have a weak spot for kids and animals.

Odd. The guard calls a few names. I push forward to inform the guard I'm hearing impaired and cannot hear the names he's calling. He repiles. "I don't give a fuck, get back"

I wait with strained ears and finally hear my name called. I fill out most of the form and am horrified to see that in-house arrest must take place in a home in the same county as the jail. Everyone I know lives in the adjacent county...I'm fucked. The prisoners who are not approved are stripped again, searched again and returned to their dorm.

When I get back to the dorm I see a new guy in the middle row. He's laying down and looking dope sick. The rest of the day passes slowly. Night arrives and I'm surprised to see a leader from the other gang get up on deck and demand everyone's attention. I sit up in my bunk to maximize my chances of actually understanding what he's saying. He starts yelling and pointing in my general direction. 'What the fuck?' Why is this guy pointing at me?

I ask the guy next to me what he's saying and if the gang leader is talking about me. He replies no the 'boss' is talking about the new arrival. Apparently the guy refused to take a shower after his processing. Bad mistake. I lay down to sleep and the next morning wake to find the guy isn't there. I don't ask why.

DAY 4

My name is called first thing in the morning. I dare to hope against all odds that I'm finally getting the fuck out of here. The dorm has become increasingly tense over the last couple days. Tension between the gangs? I'm crushed when I'm transferred to a new dorm. Same setup, two new gangs. These are mostly Hispanic gang bangers. I'm given a blanket and a book when I ask for a guy's help filling out the commissary form. Ha, even in this place money is power. I tell him to pick an item or two off the list in exchange for his help. He chooses five. No big deal. Knowledge can make the difference between life and death in this place. Gotta know the rules and have someone watching your back, so I agree. The day passes much more quickly and I devour the book. It's actually quite good. A thriller type of book. I wish I could remember the title. Some things best left alone I guess.

DAY 5

The next morning my name is called but I do not hear the guard. My new friend gives me a nudge and says 'Hurry up, man, you're going home'. I'm dumbfounded. I think I actually grinned. I give the guy my blanket, book and the small surplus of smokes I've aquired and quickly walk out of the room. After hours of processing, I'm released. I walk, almost run, out of the jail feeling born again. I hustle to the hot dog stand outside the jail and order a coke and a hot dog. Nothing ever tasted better. It was only five days in that place, but let me tell you, five days without knowing when you're being released is an eternity. I enroll in an intensive outpatient rehab in my neighborhood and begin my long journey to sobriety. With my family's help I hire a lawyer and fight the over-inflated charges for over a year. I'm victorious eventually and am fined, given community service, lose my driver's license and put on probation for a year. Not too bad seeing as how I was facing 4-12 in the slammer.

AFTERTHOUGHT

So, a few thoughts on closing. I've successfully completed my probation, my rehab, getting my license back and am sober now almost four years. It's still very difficult trying to find gainful employment with a felony on my record. The things we take for granted huh? The last 10 years of my life wasted, all the time and money spent and for what? A twenty dollar piece of cocaine. Funny thing is I didn't know controlled substances were a felony. Even an empty seal with residue on it is a class four felony. Instead of the asinine commercials and propaganda and 'just say no' anti-drug slogans why not inform the public of the very real dangers and consequences of hard drug use? The only answer I come up with is there's big money in incarceration.

A few things I've learned in my time spent on that dark path of pain that is hard drug use. You cannot help a person who doesn't want to be helped. This I can attest to having been through it.

The alcohol/drug abuser/addict must hit bottom before they can piece their life back together, if ever.

A person MUST have some sort of support group in their struggle to get/stay sober. Especially if they're new to sobriety. In my opinion It doesn't necessarily have to be 'god' oriented but certainly positively driven.

Positive hobbies/alternative are VERY important.

People and places. This was MY shtick. An alcoholic cannot hang in bars, a drug abuser/addict cannot hang with people who use. Period. While it's hard to find new friends I guarantee you if/when you get caught (And they/we all do) your friends will be chosen for you in jail/prison.

When an employer does a background check the charges a person has NOT the convictions is displayed. So I guess that D.A. won after all. I am not nor was I ever a drug dealer but to prospective employers, according to my home state/background check, I was.

I've been out of work a long time now. I refuse to give up though. I'll be damned if I EVER have to be strip searched, humiliated and put in harm's way courtesy of the system that occurs daily. I will never again be treated like an animal due to a consequence of my making...

Ever again.... It just isn't worth it.

Hope you've enjoyed my story. Hope I helped someone out there. Hope...Very important to the perspective sober human being. Good luck to you.

CPSIA information can be obtained at www.ICGtesting.com
Printed in the USA
LVOW040220180512

282140LV00002B/157/P